LAUGH OUT LOUD

ANIMALS

By Jeffrey Burton

LITTLE SIMON
New York London Toronto Sydney New Delhi

LITTLE SIMON
An imprint of Simon & Schuster Children's Publishing Division
1230 Avenue of the Americas, New York, New York 10020
First Little Simon edition April 2017

Designed by Brittany Naundorff
Manufactured in China 0217 QUL
10 9 8 7 6 5 4 3 2
ISBN 978-1-4814-8117-5 (pbk)
ISBN 978-1-4814-8118-2 (eBook)

Welcome and get ready to **LAUGH OUT LOUD** with this **Animal Meme Joke Book** that's out to prove once and for all that wildlife are the funniest critters on earth.

Before you start, here are some helpful tips to make this book even funnier:

- give each animal its own special voice
- give each joke its own special delivery
- make sure you share the best jokes with your friends
- and don't be afraid to make up your own jokes, too!

MONKEY FACT:

The one who smelt it, *dealt it.*

one Puppissippi,
two Puppissippi, three Puppissippi...

BOB'S FINALLY
COMING OUT OF
HIS SHELL.

Excuse me.

You gonna EAT that?

WHO YOU CALLIN'

CHEETAHS?!

Oh deer, did I forget my lunch box again?

I regret to inform you that I am not

MOOOOOO -ving.

Picture day did not go well for Little Kitty Paws.

Squirrrrr rrrrelll,

that's my

JAM!

Should pigs fly? Hmm . . .

Prairie dogs are cooler than regular dogs. Pass it on!

How zebras laugh:

ZEE-

HA

A

BRAH-HA-HA!
HA-HA-HA-HA!
HA-HA-HA
A-HA-HA-H
HAHA-HAHA-
HA-HA!
HAHA-HA-HA-HA!

MY PEOPLE NEED ME.

I'VE FALLEN AND I
PANDA GET UP!

I'm
kanga-ROOT-ing
for you.

POLLY REALLY WANTED A CRACKER.

IS IT A LITTLE FROGGY OUT?
OR IS IT JUST ME?

CHEESE BOOGERS

All I said was "Red's not your color!"

We shouldn't have eaten that last slice of **homework.**

woof.

GNARLY AIRWALK,

TINY TURTLE!

I HEARD MEOWZART
WROTE SONGS ABOUT FELINES.

THE DOG DID IT.

Look **deep** into my eyes . . .

you are getting
very sleeeeepy.

This was a fur real bad idea. . . .

WHEN YOUR BROTHER GETS EXTRA SCREEN TIME . . .

what do I do
meow?

Rhino what to do . . .

JUMP!

SLOOOOOW and

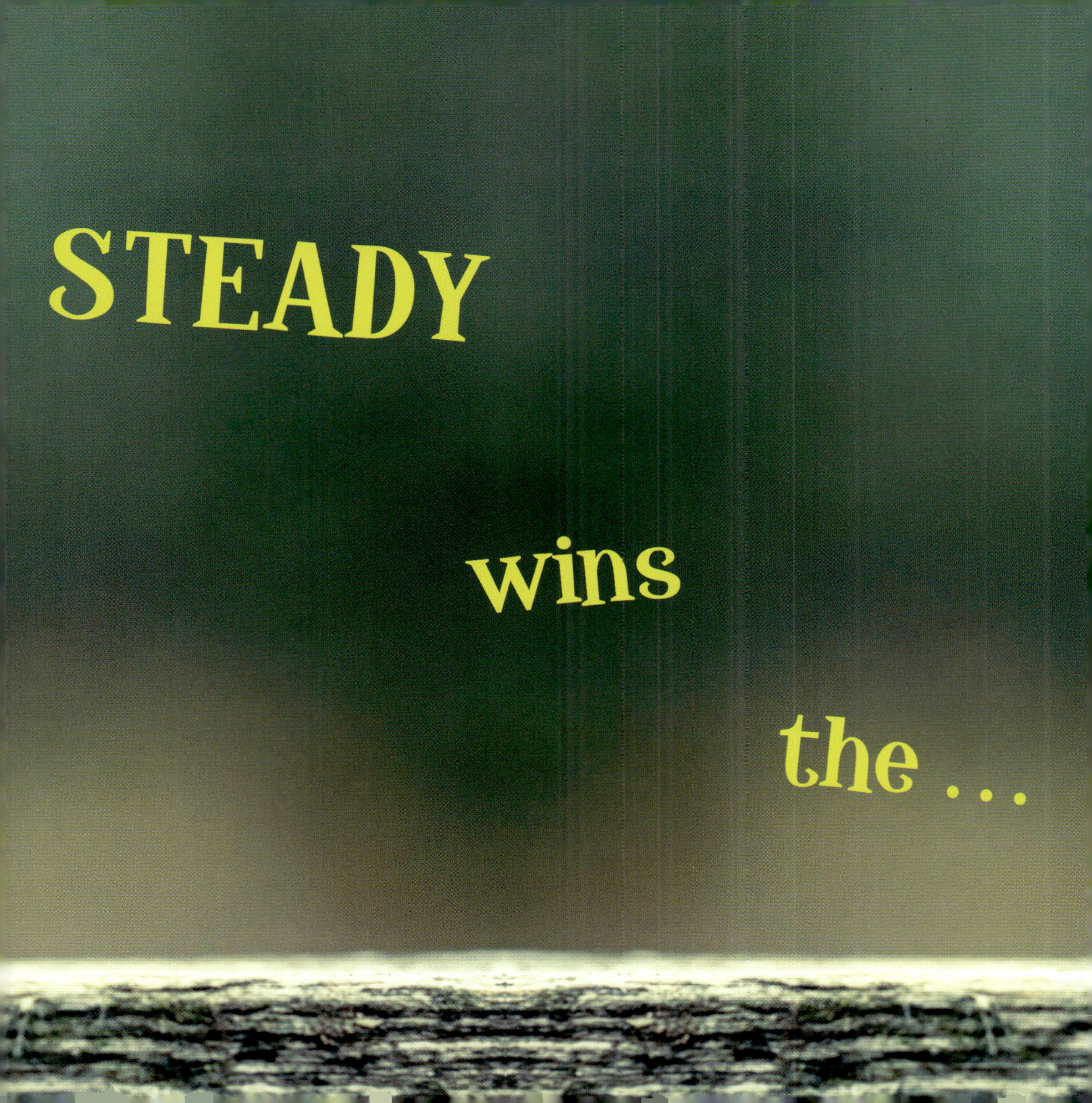

STEADY

wins

the . . .

FEED ME

RIGHT MEOW

DRAMATIC. PENGUIN.
SLO-MO. WALK.

OSTRICH
EVERY MORNING.

IGUANA MAKE YOU LAUGH

HORSE CHEESE

WAIT . . .
DO THEY
PUT CATS
IN CATNIP?!

Talk to me
I'M ALL EARS

AM I COOL YET?

SHH . . .
I'M HIDING

YOU'LL NEVER GUESS
WHAT THE COW HERD.

awkward.

IF I FITS, I SITS.

DON'T JUST TRY IT,
GO-PHER
IT!

That's so
SEALY!!!

HOO
HOO
HOO

you
talkin'
to?

I CAN'T OPEN IT!

You're a **slippery** one, Tweeters.

I CAN SEE YOU

THIS
HAIRSTYLE
MAKES
ME LOOK
300
DOG YEARS
YOUNGER.

You had *one job*, Carl!

ONE JOB.

MONKEY FACT:
it hurts when I do this.
(Don't do that.)

DID YOU SAY CAR RIDE?!

THE MOUSEHAT WAS
NOT STEVE'S STYLE.

STEVE, YOUR HAT IS FREAKING ME-OWT.

Raise your hand
if you ate too much
honey!

Meow you see me,
meow you don't!

SUP?

THE FISH
WAS

THIS BIG!

I SWEAR!

DOG BUSINESS 101:

Grandma sent me another sweater . . .

the dog party was
OFF THE LEASH!

When you realize there's

no school

on Monday.

Are you **KID-DING** me?

YOUR MOVE, HUMAN.

Fred caught the UFO and saved all dog-kind.

WHEN MOM COMBS
YOUR HAIR

THE SHOW MUST GO PAW-N

I'M A WIZARD.

The hills are alive
with the sound of
MOOOOO-sic

Don't tell me . . .

the ribbon is back!

I MEAN BUSINESS
MONKEY BUSINESS

TAKE A BATH, THEY SAID

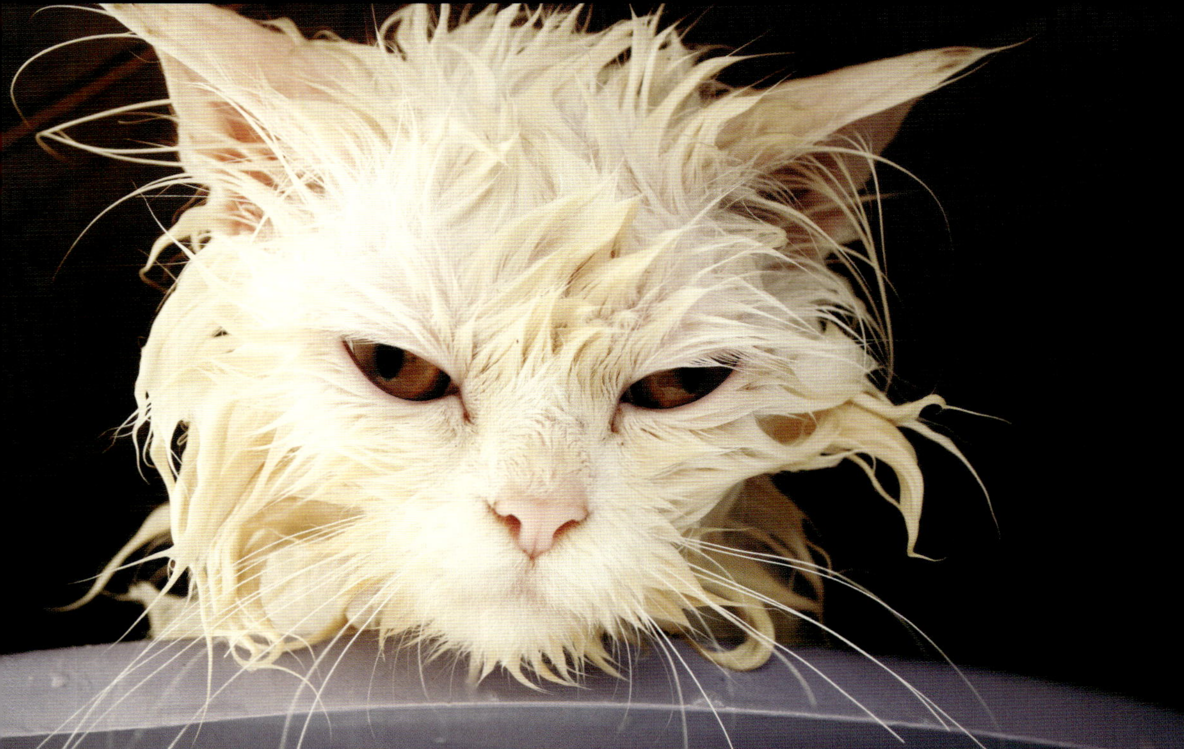

IT'LL BE FUN, THEY SAID

LLAMA DRAMA!

ALL NINE LIVES FLASHED BEFORE WHISKERS' EYES.

IS DRESSING UP YOUR CAT A GOOD IDEA?

WHEN THE BARBER ASKS IF YOU LIKE YOUR NEW HAIRCUT

You think I'm cute?
Aww, get otter here!

Sooooooo tired . . .

Only slept for 21 hours.

Wait, you made banana bread?

YOU'RE WEARING
THAT AGAIN?

I give up,
cat wins.

THE KITTENS KNOW WHAT YOU DID.

Is this organic?

THIS "PAIR-OF-KEETS" JOKE
HAS GONE TOO FAR, LENNY!

COWABUNGA, DUDE!

JUST SAY NO to yellow snow.

I am definitely **NOT** a flying squirrel.

EXCUSE ME, YOU GONNA EAT THAT?

AND THEN SHE PUT THE
DOG IN TIME-OUT!

BOW-WOW DOWN
TO YOUR KING AND QUEEN.

This flower

stinks.

They thought they could give him a bath . . .

Talk
to the
PAW

MOM!!!
I CAN'T FIND
MY SHOES!!

I don't always
look this good,
but when I do,
everyone goes
bananas!

The dancing lemur waits for no one.

CHA-CHA-CHA!

I'm afraid it's bad news . . .
You're a cat.

HE HAS THE TREAT.

GIVE US THE TREAT.

MY HUGS ARE THE

BEST KOALA-TY

Swan says WHAAA?

My lips are
SEALED

DRop the food,
human. DRop the
food.

So this is the other side? Boring!

DAAAAAD!!
I can't find my TOOTHBRUSH!!

THE BIRDS. THEY TEASE ME.

NO.
THIS IS NOT A WIG.

DON'T LOOK!

(I'm neigh-ked!)

DEEP IN HIS BURROW,
FURBALL PLOTS HIS REVENGE.

NO
SCHOOL
TODAY!!

MEOW?
MORE LIKE ME-WOW!

Hey! Who burped in the pool?

CAT-IN-THE-BOX!

JAZZ
HANDS!

I AM NOT
AN ARMADILLO.

Come in!
The water's fine!

MONDAYS

GOT ME LIKE . . .

Homework
is for the
BIRDS

Hmmmm . . .
this food is invisible.

HEYYY GIRL

TREE-
HUGGER.

Hola,

SOY PARROT.

DANCE
LIKE
NO ONE'S
WATCHING!

SO!
MUCH!
BAMBOO!!

You're just jelly,
this hat is
CLAW-some!

Go Guinea, it's your

BIRTHDAY

I ATE THE Easter Bunny

I HOPE
YOU'RE
SHOPPING
FOR MORE
CATNIP

Just wait,
I'm going to be a

Beautiful Batterfly

Drool-free guarantee!
Welcome to
DOGSMART

Your art
stinks.

HELP!
IT'S A
MOUSE!

POOP OR TREAT

CAN YOU
HANDLE THE
PUG LIFE?

LEAF!

YUCK!
DOG BREATH.

HOVER PUPPY!

POLAR BROS

4 LIFE!

AWKWARD.

I'm not
DONNER,
I'm BLiTZEN

THE KOALA KNOWS
WHAT YOU DID.

Have you seen my duck?

THE CAT DID IT.

I LEFT YOU A PRESENT.

Put your
PAWS
where
I can
SEE 'EM!

UP! UP!
And away!

I DON'T SEE ANY FRENCH FRIES*...

BET WE LOOK

AWESOME

DOING THIS SYNCHRONIZED SWIMMING THING, LARRY.

TONIGHT,
WE FEAST.

IT'S DOG,
JAMES DOG.

Are you
a prince?

THAT JOKE WAS
UNBEARABLE.

UHHH... I THINK I PUMA PANTS....

OH NO SHE DI-IN'T.

GASP!
I've been
SPOTTED!

GRRRRRL, fleas!

Duck . . .

Duck . . .

GOOSE!!

Unhand me,
villain!

It's a bird! It's a plane!

IT'S A BAAAA.

AAALL!!

WHO ARE YOU CALLIN' CHICKEN?

I got it . . . I got it . . .
I don't got it.

What?
He woke me from my cat nap.

OH MEOW GOSH!
YUMMERZ!!

I like to knit.

WE ATTACK
AT DAWN!

We will spare no dogs, sir.

KING PUPPY
REQUIRES A BONE.

If you wanted french fries SO BAD, Hank . . .
you should have just ordered them yourself!!

WAAAAAAZZZZZ-
UUUPPPPP!

COOKiES?
What cookies?
I'm innocent!

DACHSHUND
THROUGH THE SNOW ...

HOW COME THE MOUSE
NEVER CHASES ME?

It's a

GOOSE

WILD
CHASE!

IT'S RAINING CATS AND DOGS?

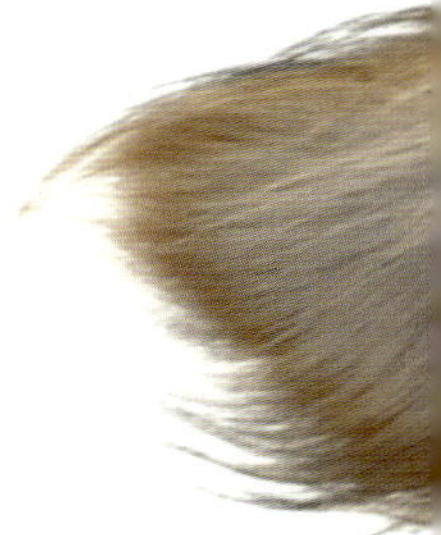

That sounds terrible.

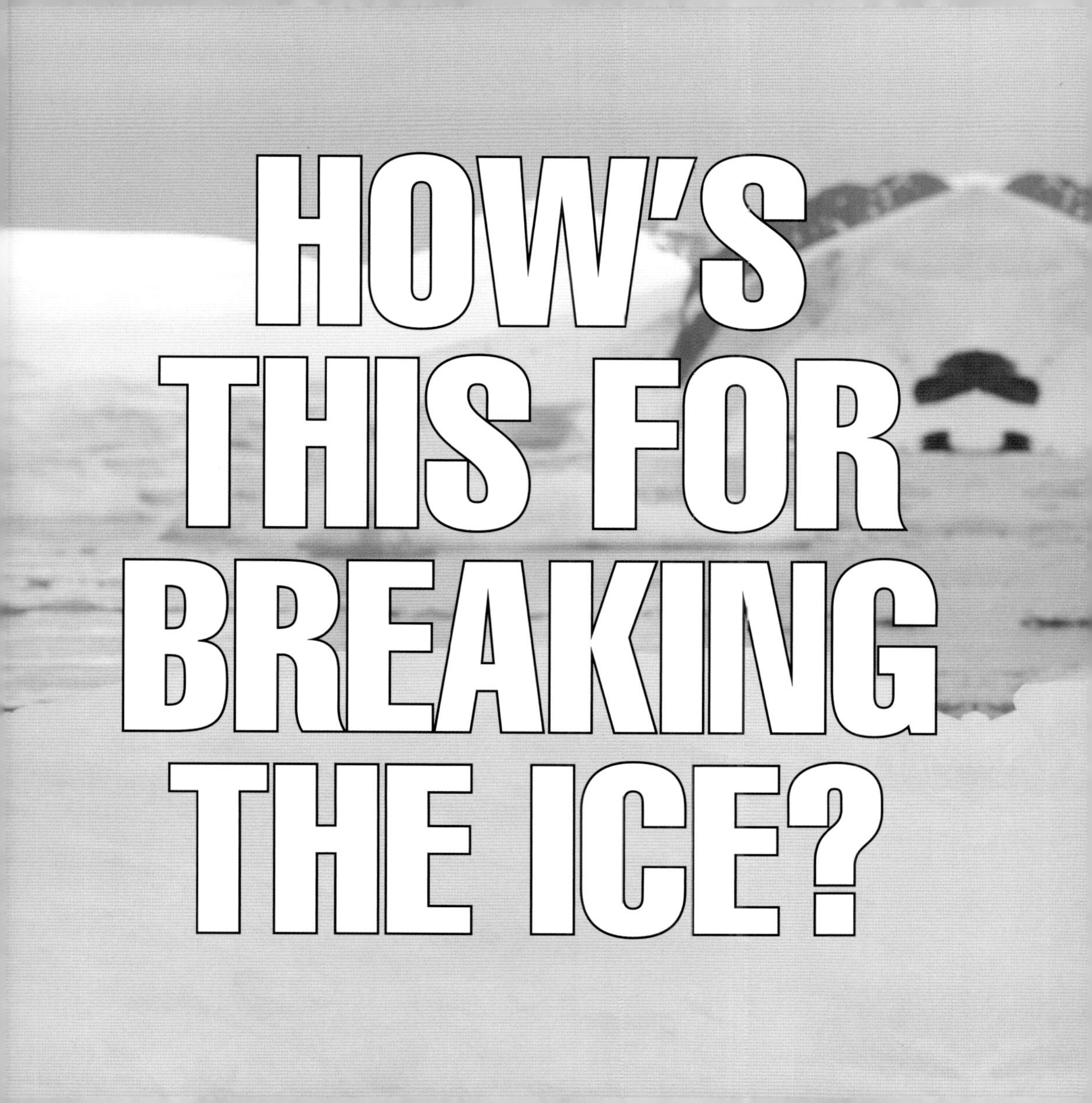
HOW'S
THIS FOR
BREAKING
THE ICE?

GROSS!!

Timmy peed in the pool

AGAIN!

I said
LEMUR
me alone!

for you, my love.

Yes, ‘twas I who stole the toilet paper.

HEY!
WHAT'S THE
PIG IDEA?!

Meow YOU doin'?

CHILL OUT,
I GOT THIS.

YOU QUACK ME UP!